M

Gypsy

Poetry and Prose

Melody Lee

Copyright © 2017 Melody Lee

Editor: Lauren Davis

Cover Design: Melody Lee

First Edition

ISBN-13: 978-1535297097

ISBN-10: 1535297093

DEDICATION

Dedicated to all gypsy warrior spirits roaming the Earth and to all Electric Birds discovering their magic wings. And for those who still believe in impossible dreams.

You are the love behind all my poems,
The wild in my writing,
The golden path of stars lighting my heart.
This love has become magic and art.

CONTENTS

INTRODUCTION

Woven in my words is an enchanting love story, the story of humans, brilliantly and beautifully created, full of flaws, full of perfections...filled with every color in the spectrum, including dark. It's the story of knowing ourselves, of being in touch not only with the light and the vivacious, but also the blue, the solemn and the melancholy; all our brokenness, all our completeness. If I can gracefully convey the purity of loving all our parts and pieces, then I have succeeded in delivering soulful inspiration through poetry and prose, through words, emotions, and loving vibrations. This to me is magic and moonlight.

Aside from my own mad tenacity, my compulsive need to write, I wish to inspire you to love YOU. Open your mind to infinite possibilities and discover your glorious wings. Find the magic harbored within all of us.

I Write

I write

because my soul speaks to me

in ways

I would not otherwise hear.

I write

because I thirst.

I write

because I hunger.

I write

because I know

of no other way

to quench the longing

deep within my being.

I write...because I must.

Wordsmiths

Even when we are not writing we're writing...scribbling thoughts in our heads...oh, if you could take a tour of my mind...if you could take a ride down the long tunnel of my maddening heart. Even when we're not creating there are words wiggling in our brains...it never turns off, never shuts down...doesn't go to sleep or take vacations...it just keeps spinning like the earth, burning like the sun.

I swear that girl was born
with a pen in her hand,
the moon in her hair
and stars in her soul.

Her Skin

Her skin

smells

of vintage books

and pale moonlight

Exotic things

Forbidden loves

and rainy nights.

Pieces of Her

You will find pieces of her
in everything you thought
you left behind. In the eye
of the storm, you will see her.
In the wind, you will hear her.
In the rain, you will touch her.
For she is the earth beneath
your feet, the air you breathe,
the love you desperately need.

Angels and Demons

The lunatic obsessed

with the moon,

like the mad girl

obsessed with the edge...

We all have our demons

that tantalize us in the light,

and angels that save us

from drowning in the night.

Synchronicity

It was no mere accident
you were sent to me,
perfect synchronicity.
Familiar souls
wrapped in skin,
brought together
through time again.

Epitome of Art

You are strange

A deep sea of mystery

Tangled mix of starlight and darkness

A beautiful mess, and I am devastatingly drawn

To every curve of your mind

Every dark scar on your body

You are the epitome of art -

Dynamic,

Strange and beautiful.

Internal Dance

If you see her staring into space,

probably her mind is in a deep poetic embrace

or a story is brewing in that clever little head.

The girl is in a trance,

it will pass—

Just let her be until she has completed

her dazzling internal dance.

Lost in the Sky

Try not to be dismayed if you find her

dancing under a blazing afternoon sun.

She cares not who sees her or what they think,

she's preoccupied with feeling the wind twisting in her

hair and embracing the earth beneath bare feet.

You see, she carries the weight of the world on her back.

To lose herself in the sky for a time is how

this free-spirited girl survives.

Falling in Love

She's not stumbling,

she's not lost.

She's simply romancing

her inner animal

and falling in love

with the wild part of her soul.

Unleashing

In creating, we unlock something deep within ourselves.

Creating is cathartic, it's freeing.

The key is to unleash your savage soul creativity,

break wide open the bonds of captivity.

You opened parts of me I didn't know existed;
now birds keep flying out...

Interior of Your Soul

I am not searching for peace.

I'm searching for art, and art is messy,

art is rebellious, art is chaotic.

I do not desire clean and tidy.

I want your scars,

your darkness,

your secrets.

I want to see the

interior of your soul.

Writers

Writers, poets, artists,

eccentrics, even if they

appear tame, have wild souls.

They just do and trying

to remove that part of them

is like caging or clipping a bird's wings.

You might stop the bird from flying,

but it will always fly given the chance.

It's innate; a wild soul will always be wild,

no matter the attempt to tame it,

and that is actually

quite beautiful.

To Know Her

If you want to know her

Study her soul:

Read her favorite books

Explore poets she admires

Listen to her favorite songs

Learn about the stars,

the oceans

and beautifully wild things.

Emitting Love

He tried to be my moon, but the stars would not allow.

I thought he could be my sun, but he did not know how.

Now I'm all alone howling in the wind,

floating in the clouds,

praising the Universe for what She knew all along.

I was meant to be a lone warrior wolf,

emitting love and light to those more in need.

Orchids and Moonlight

Don't compare her
to sunshine and roses
when she's clearly
orchids and moonlight.

Blue Butterflies and Black Widows

She's into blue butterflies and black widows

Angels and spiritual things

Freedom and the open road

Solitude and thunderstorms

She's into authentic hearts and

Mind shattering conversations

Good music and quirky art

Weirdness and eccentric people

Love, kindness and genuine souls

She's into all this and so much more.

How to Start a Revolution

Begin by being true to your heart. Listen to the sweet song of your soul. Immediately, stop marching to the dull beat of the herd and start vibing to your own unique, vivacious heartbeat.

Cease this instant trying to fit into a mold. Trying to be part of the crowd is not for someone who was born to stand out, stand tall and shine. Remember, you won't fly to great heights with clipped wings or by growing the same feathers as the flock. You are meant to fly higher! Made to sparkle in the sky! You are not and will never be ordinary. And thank God you don't fit in that bland square box. Shine your diamond moonlight to the world. Honor your fabulous flaws. You are perfectly imperfect...the zigzag in a straight line, a rainbow in a world of clouds. Ditch your fears and be the rebel wolf queen you inherently are! And this, this is how you start a revolution!

Spitfire

Don't tell a girl with fire in her veins
and hurricane bones
what she should and shouldn't do.
In the blink of an eye,
she will shatter that ridiculous cage
you attempt to build around her
beautiful bohemian spirit.

She's a dark-eyed,
red flame,
bohemian
hurricane.

I am a wildflower in your perfect bed of roses.

Wildflowers

can't be controlled,

and neither can the girl

with a soul boundless

as the sky,

and a spirit as free

and wild as the ocean.

What some label as crazy, those with intuitive souls, artistic spirits and open minds call PASSION.

You shouldn't expect a pretty

little thing like her

to sit still.

She has wings the color of wild

and a soul the color of art.

She was never meant to be contained.

Never meant to be caged.

Wolves

Trust your wolf instincts.

Use the power of your intelligence

for the betterment of you and your world.

Know your worth, because it's fucking awesome!

Speak to yourself in love, daily and often.

Love yourself – that amazing badass woman or man.

Be witty. Laugh often. Laugh at yourself.

Don't take shit from anyone.

Be clear about this: Your heart is a wolf.

Fierce.

Loyal.

Loving.

And wolves don't eat bullshit.

You are nothing less than a Masterpiece.

Inner Voice

If it doesn't feel right to the heart, then it's not right for the soul. Listen to the beat of what you instinctively know. Let that inner voice be your guide. Follow and obey, because the truth of the matter is while the brain staggers, plays tricks, gets confused, the heart, the soul ... they do not lie; they know the way.

When you are lost in the right way,
you don't go back to being found in the wrong way.

Dance

Dance with those who embrace your insanity,

your passionate spirit, your artistic expressions.

These are your kindred souls;

they will not only encourage you to fly,

they will fly with you.

Leave those who inhibit your mad creativity

and hinder your wild side.

Wish them well, but they aren't your tribe.

Anything that empties you, empty it.

You are far too precious to be anything

but filled with life, love,

full of goodness and wild adventures.

You are Queen of Love. Warrior of Light.

Fill your cup accordingly.

Life is too short for anything less.

Moon Gypsy

She's the kind of girl

who brings you to the moon

without you even being aware.

The kind of girl you trip into love with.

The kind of girl you never forget.

Soul Sex

I could

make love

with you

until the

moon decides

to never

glow again.

Old Time Charm

Coffee shops

Paris cafes

Decadent things

Always perk her up,

For she is a lover

Of old time charm

Poetry and art

An exotic eccentric

At heart.

Hollow

Some people have hollow souls.
They'll see your light and like a moth
to a flame, they'll gravitate toward you.
Be cautious, for these souls will attempt
to steal your joy and try robbing
the sparkle from your eyes.

Warrior Gloves

It's a confused world.

Some days beautiful.

Other days, brutally unkind.

But you...you keep your world kind.

Let no sourpuss downer dull your shine.

Wear your warrior gloves,

your heart love and walk proudly

with that crazy sweet twinkle in your eyes.

Every. Single. Day.

Rules

Rules I follow:

My heart

What I listen to:

My Soul

What I see:

A person's soul

Wild Thing

Don't try figuring her out,

she's not meant to be solved.

Once you think you have her decoded

she'll go and change course.

And don't try putting her together;

she's not a puzzle.

Love her for the chaotic

beautiful mess she is.

Love her in the moment and let

the Universe take care of the rest.

She is a wild thing and will

remain that way until the end.

Gypsy Flower

Gypsy flower, own your wild.

To be a free spirit is beautiful and brave.

To claim your wings is courageous.

You are freedom.

You are inspiration.

Allow your roots to shine, bloom and energize

into the magnificence that you are.

Feel the strength of your budding wings,

while your petals silently draw in love.

The Not-So-Secret Secret

It's not a crime to love too much, to overload your soul with pure bliss, to love with maddening abandon. The crime is in holding back, barricading your heart, preventing the natural flow of love, life. Freedom is in removing the barriers and allowing yourself to become vulnerable, to feel at the very depths of your core. Sure, love is a risk, but isn't it better to risk and find life, then to become numb and find death? Without love, life is meaningless. This is the magic and not-so-secret secret of the Universe.

Remove the mask.
Let me love the darkness you hide underneath.

Thirst

I inhale his skin as he breathes in my light.

We are the counterpart of each other.

When he is darkness, I bring him fire.

When I the sun, he brings me his sea.

We drink in each other as the ocean drinks in salt,

as the desert thirsts for liquid gold,

as vampires crave the bite!

He was rich in gold;
not the material kind,
the spiritual, soulful kind.

Exquisite Little Stars

I want to dip into your beautiful scars,

learn their stories.

I want to trace them with my fingertips,

kiss them with my heart,

write them into poetry

and turn them all into exquisite little stars.

Human

You're human. You can't be a "motivational speaker" every damn day of your life. It's okay to have dark days. Allow yourself to go there, then come back up with a gusto, like you always do. You're an angel, but you're also human. Don't beat yourself up for being authentic.

Hug your soul once in a while;
It deserves the love you're so busy giving everyone else.

Touch

My soul

must reach

into the clouds

and touch

the beauty

of madness.

Sometimes a girl just craves a little danger.

Strange and Unusual

I have an attraction to strange

and unusual things.

I find them interesting,

spellbinding,

utterly fascinating.

Dangerous, Beautiful Darkness

Her skin smelled like the twilight moon

and her eyes looked primal,

like a hungry animal.

She was darkness –

dangerous, beautiful darkness.

Her blood is made of moonlight;
part dark, part light.

Beast and Beauty

There is a beast

within my heart.

She plays immaculately

with the beauty in my soul.

She has one hell of a dark soul,
but damn,
it's so full of light!

Fairytales

She adored fairy tales,

yet derived great reward

rewriting them to the melody of her own warrior soul.

Her fairytales weren't made of desperate girls

being rescued by handsome

spoiled princes.

Her stories were made of badass women

teasing monsters

and running wild with dragons.

Belle of the Night

The moon glistens

in her dreamy eyes

as she frolics in the dark forest.

She's got wild overgrowing in her bones,

and tangles upon tangles of midnight

weaving through her long silky hair,

this belle of the night.

She's always been a wild forest,
a creature of the night.

Magic

Don't rule out magic in ordinary things.

Simply open your heart

Expand your mind

and believe.

Magic is all around;

it can be felt in raindrops touching your cheeks

and seen in rainbows after a storm.

Falling in love is also a magical thing.

Why is it so difficult to believe in magic?
Do you not believe in love?

Rebel Animal, Heart Overflowing

She's over the top rebellious,

but damn her heart

overflowing with insane love.

She shakes thing up.

Doesn't play by rules and certainly fits

in nobody's pretty perfect box.

Mad Ones

Groomed and clean cut are fine and dandy,

but I want to run with the mad ones;

the ones comfortable playing in overgrown forests,

rolling in leaves,

dancing under a scorching sun.

The ones not afraid of getting dirty.

Not afraid of burning.

More than Skin

I am skin,

but underneath lives

fire and stars and wild!

Paths

We walk different paths. Don't try being like someone else, you are uniquely you. And don't judge others for the paths they've chosen. There are no wrong ways, merely different ways. Maybe some slower, others quicker, but they all journey...somewhere! Even wrong turns lead somewhere and stumbling blocks lead to learning. I've made what seem like poor choices at certain times in my life, haven't we all, but we made it through and we are usually better, stronger, wiser for the choices that perhaps once seemed terribly wrong, but in the grand scheme of life, they were absolutely right! Even if we don't understand that now.

Don't walk my path,
I won't walk yours.
Maybe we'll meet somewhere in the middle,
but your journey and my journey
are not the same;
what a bland world this would it be
if they were.

A Twist on Kindness

Kindness

is never weakness

if it has potential

to cause death.

So, if you can

"kill them with kindness,"

the ball is in your court.

YOU have the power!

Shower the darkness with love
and watch light illuminate.

I Belong

I belong with the trees,

the wind,

the earth beneath my feet.

I belong in the land of enchanting things.

But mostly,

I belong entwined in your kiss,

lost,

yet wild and free,

pure bliss,

like poetry.

Hope Droplets

She doesn't burn bridges,

she covers them in gypsy flowers

and feather kisses,

then strolls along her merry way.

Too heavy to carry grudges,

she leaves love and hope droplets

wherever she goes.

Too much war, hatred and fear in the world.
Desperately needed:
More art, love and poetry.

Internal Tattoo

While they all ink their skin,

I crave something permanent within.

Bare your soul

Open your heart

Tattoo your love within.

Run Away with Me

Don't want a complicated love.

Just want you to grab my demons,

Kiss my madness

and run away

with me.

Broken

You broke me

I'm trying

to put all

the pieces

back together

The process

is taking

longer

than expected.

~ Lost ~
If falling for you meant losing myself,
I'd gladly get lost all over again.
You were the sweetest forbidden fruit,
the juiciest sin ~
Let's do it all again.

Wild Hearts

Those with wild hearts love big

Love fiercely

Love with every fiber

of their feral being.

Collision

Once our souls collided and caught fire,

there was no turning back.

Love is a collision of two stars,

it's as simple and as complicated as that.

Love flares up like fire and stars and rockets!

Best Loves

The best loves are strange loves,
woven with beautiful scars,
peculiar darkness
and exquisite hearts.

Vibrational Pull

The vibrational pull of

two synchronized hearts

find their way through

the storms,

the cosmos

and back

to each other.

Lost

You're only lost
because you're searching
for the other half
of your soul.

Losing myself led me to the truth of my soul.

Moon Gypsy II

The gypsy

in her

loved

the wolf

in him.

Sweet angel by day
Wild animal by night

I Love You

I love you just as you are

All your funky flaws and gorgeous imperfections

Your crazy mannerisms

Your wit

Your clever mind

Your dark scars and bright eyes

I love the way you love me

Even when my sky is black you hold my hand

And never let go

You're magnetic just as you are

The star in my heart

I love you.

Home

While they all stumbled

over her exotic looks,

he felt a familiar comfort

in her tangled hair,

an unexpected warmth

in her presence.

He saw the animal in her eyes

and knew he found home.

He embraced the fire spirit in her soul.

And she embraced him.

Together their souls

fell in mad love.

Together they were home.

Together they were free.

Connections

Whiskey and wine,

late night dates.

Favorite books,

heated debates,

Witty banter,

deep belly laughs.

These are the kind of soul connections

I'm talking about.

Next morning:
Coffee, no wi-fi, soft blankets,
making magic with you!
A girl can dream.

Personal Evolution

Some people are so fearful and caged

they never allow the fragrance of love to enter.

How sad to give fear that much power,

blocking infinite possibilities.

Stop living in your own inflicted cage.

A cage of thought, a cage of what

others want or expect you to be.

A prison of your own making.

Open latch and free yourself.

The only thing staying behind the door does is

hinder your personal evolvement.

~ Fly ~
Didn't realize the abundance of birds inside me,
until you hijacked the key
I kept so closely guarded to my heart.

Bird in My Chest

The beak of the bird in my chest

pecks and gnaws,

occasionally sings,

frequently jabs.

It rips, it bites, it stabs

The bird, the bird,

trapped in the cage of my ribs.

Release

And in the letting go
I found more freedom
than I could have ever
possibly imagined.
The refusal to release
what no longer served
my soul only enslaved me.
Release the fear of letting go.
Release what holds you captive.

Scenic Route

She knows precisely where she's going,

she's just taking the scenic route there.

Important to savor the journey,

and at this point in her life

she understands that more than ever.

Sashay

Take my hand

Let's sashay

under the moon

Chase stars

and get lost

in the night.

~ Stars ~
I love the stars.
They always find a way
to pull me away.

Dreamer Girl

She's just a girl

who dreams

too deeply

for this world.

Sometimes
a girl just needs to soak
in a hot bath
full of petals
and forget the world for a bit.

Bohemian Queen

Poetic eyes, goddess-like,

and a starlight soul.

She's a bohemian queen

with a warrior's heart of gold.

With fervor and fire,

she diligently fights for the underdog,

her secret wolf pack.

She loves the darling sinners

and adoringly welcomes the vagabonds,

wayward ones, poets, writers,

artists ... the roaming gypsy souls.

These kindred spirits are her tribe,

her heart's vibe.

Wild

There's no returning from the wild.

Wild things stay with you,

residing in your spirit,

pulsing in your veins.

Wild may try hiding,

but never truly goes away.

Wild shows up in her messy hair,

her sassy smile, the glimmer in her eyes.

It's in her craving for the moon

and the way she connects with nature and the wind.

The way she unabashedly

goes skinny dipping on a whim.

Wild is the way she mourns at cruelty and inhumanity.

How she howls when beloved animals

are hunted for profit or sport.

Wild is in her hungry kiss, her savage sex.

Wild is in the blood and bones;

it doesn't go away.

Nocturnal Creature

The darkness is her rainbow

The night a place to shine

For this nocturnal creature

Comes undone when the black

Of the sky caresses

The base of her spine.

*Sometimes the only way to find your light is to crawl around
in the dark. Then, share your light with the world.
Spread that star stuff everywhere you go!*

Extraordinary Love

An extraordinary love
is like an eagle in flight:
Powerful, divine,
unafraid and unrestrained.
Rooted in spirit and freedom,
entwined like earth and wind.

Exploration

It's not just about exploring your body-

It's about exploring your thoughts

Your mind

What makes you roar

What makes you shine.

I like your mind when it plays with mine.
We harmonize like a dirty sweet symphony.

Propellers

Your invisible wings represent visible courage.

Bravery. Freedom.

Not stagnation, complacency or fear.

Put those vibrant propellers to use.

Limit the downward,

look upward

and take flight!

The sky is waiting for you

and the Universe demands it.

Rebel Art

With poetry,

rules are meant to be broken.

And that's the beauty of poetry;

it's rebellious,

like me.

Spikes and Fangs

I am not a behind-the-desk,

away-from-natural-light kind of gal.

Confinement and control

are not my cup of tea;

the two simply don't agree with me

and my raven wolf heart.

My winged spirit is allergic to both.

My soul craves things that fly,

that soar, that run wild and free

Don't try taming me,

I'll end up growing spikes on my wings

and fangs in my mouth.

Royal Flower

Wildflower,

Flame flower,

Tropaeolum speciosum,

the one standing freely,

majestically,

proud and unafraid

in a field of gold.

The Wild Flame Flower,

SHE is the real royalty.

Stay rooted, grounded…and remember,
the best way to bloom is to love and be loved.

Guarded Eyes

Beware the ones
with guarded eyes;
they hide flames inside.
Once you break through,
you'll discover
a plethora of treasures
to behold...art, love,
adventures...exotic
and forbidden things.

Eruption

In the midst of creating

-imagining -

there is a certain madness

that erupts;

the captivating,

mysterious,

intoxicating kind.

Drunk on imagination, that's my kind of intoxication.

Let's Be Mermaids

Your soul is so bohemian,
free and gypsy wild.
Come swim with me
in the calming sea
Let's be mermaids
for a while.

When the sun goes down
we'll go ashore
and build a fire.
We'll kiss, make out,
sing lovely songs
inspired by love,
the sea
and you and me.

Caterpillar

You didn't see her before the butterfly days.

You didn't know her as the inward, awkward,

timid caterpillar.

But her vivacious wings were inevitable.

Part of her design,

her destiny.

Now you know her with a gypsy heart,

a rebel spirit.

I wonder if you'd love the dark caterpillar in her

as you love the bohemian butterfly.

I think I would suffocate without my solitude.
I'm such a loner girl, but I'm a butterfly, too.

Soul Shine

Look at your soul shine

Blowing my damn mind

Making me fall in love

all over again

with the sparkles

in your golden eyes.

Savage Love

Your savage love

My barbaric heart

Together

We'll make

The moon scream

The night howl.

Ravish her soul with love, laughter and poetry.

Chaos and Honey

She was chaos and honey

All things messy,

Sweet and lovely

Darkness entwined

With magic and stars

Supernatural,

Sacred and holy.

3 a.m.

When 3 a.m. beckons me again,

I know it's time to turn on the lamp

and pull out the pen.

The night is my secret lover,

the moon

my all-knowing friend.

Every Time We Kiss

You won't always find poetry in my words or the ink dripping off the tip of my pen. Sometimes you'll find it in the wild part of my eyes, the knots in my hair, the pulse of my heartbeat... or the way I get lost every time we kiss.

She desired only soulful things;
art, love, poetry....and his eternal kisses.

A Moment in Time

Even if it was only a moment in time,

I was yours. You were mine.

Our love, divine.

Now only memories,

some drifting into the atmosphere.

Others etched in our hearts forever.

What is Love?

If you love someone only if they love you in return, what's the point of love at all? Is not love something to freely give without thought of what you shall receive in return, or do I have love all wrong?

Love is a God quality,
and anything of that caliber of course
is powerful beyond comprehension and reasoning.

Throw Away the Damn Key

There's no possessing a wild heart

Stow away the cage

Throw away the key

Love her freely

Or let her be.

Jane

To all the prissy girls who think it's cool to wear glittery gowns and sparkly crowns, where's the adventure in that!? I'll tell you about real excitement...running barefoot in the woods, climbing trees, making forts, riding dragons. I was always Jane, minus the damsel in distress...on the hunt for Tarzan...much more fulfilling than playing dress-up.

She's a little wildflower
with a lot of warrior underneath.

Holes

You burn holes
in her heart
then wonder why
she won't return to you.

Shipwreck

Sometimes

I fail miserably

at being

the captain of my feelings,

shipwrecking my heart,

drowning the mermaid

within my soul.

Fighter

Her spirit remains strong and fierce.

You may deliver punches and throw stones.

You may bring her days of black clouds,

but bruise or break her spirit,

she will not allow.

She won't give up without a hellish fight,
don't discount that pretty face,
she has a lethal bite.

Old Soul

She's an old soul

with a Hip Hop spirit.

An old soul

craving new adventures.

When music and souls play together,
keys of love harmonize and hearts unlock.

Wolves and Warriors

Even wolves

get broken hearts

Even warriors cry.

Occasionally,
you can hear her howl,
when the sky is black
and the moon is full.

Show Me

Show me your gentleness
and I will see your strength.
Show me your rage
and I will know your weakness.

I Saw

I saw the rage in you,

the fire and hell inside

and loved you

despite it all.

What a Shame

What a shame he didn't understand

the importance of being her friend,

embracing her spirit,

crawling into her mind,

touching her soul.

She needed more than just a warm body.

If you can't stimulate her mind
it's going to be difficult to stimulate her body.
Seduction begins there, in the mind.

Lovers

Lovers are angels
until they've been hurt,
then they become monsters
and demons and dragons.

Immortal Aphrodisiacs

He loved the curves on her body,

Her soft skin and pouty lower lip,

Her deep, soulful eyes.

He adored her voice; sometimes sultry, sometimes fiery.

Her laugh, her playfulness...he adored it all.

But what really turned him on were the curves

In her mind...the twists, the turns

The fire, the brilliance

And her compassionate heart;

The beat of it harmonizing so sweetly and perfectly

With the beat of his

The whole package was beyond thrilling...

Yet her mind, her heart,

Those were the immortal aphrodisiacs.

Soul Flame

You will know he was your soul flame
by the way he treats you after a breakup.
The way he secretly takes care of you, still.
You will know if all the love he claimed
to have for you was real, or not.
His actions will prove if he was legit
or if he was a fraud.

Mask

Oops! Your mask slipped, and though I can love a beast,
I have no room for monsters and cowards claiming to be
something they're not, who lie to get what they want.

~ Eyes Speak ~
Words alone mean little.
Show me your eyes;
that's where I'll decipher
your truth from your lies.

Careful

Be careful how you treat a writer.

Her pen is her weapon,

her writing her sword.

She won't hesitate protecting those she loves,

including herself.

A writer is a warrior.
Writers write because they bleed,
because they cry;
it's how they release
all that blood
all those tears
turning them into blood
into ink
into art.

Devour

Consume Me

Spread my soul wide open

Love me there,

in the depths of my abyss

Feed my ravenous heart

Reach the animal within

Consume me.

You'll need a life preserver before diving into her soul.

Lion's Den

Don't be so lonely and desperate that you walk

smack into the lion's den.

Know your worth.

Know what you deserve.

Be cautious, don't allow yourself to be tricked.

Monsters

Monsters always play the victim.

So, ladies and gents,

be careful what you're being fed

and even more careful

what you're taking in.

Galaxy of Hope

Her eyes,

a galaxy of hope,

oh,

how they gleam

of little poems

and giant dreams.

Trouble

I could tell by his lethal eyes

and venomous kiss

I was in deep trouble,

but somehow my body

went into rebellion

logic and sense

out the window,

love and heartbreak

on the horizon.

Wolf

He smelled like a wolf
I knew I should run,
instead I opened my heart
and invited him in for a bite.

The edge of her heart
a battlefield
between love
and war.

Crawl

I wish to crawl

behind your curious eyes,

and see what you see

when you gaze into infinity.

While I chase the storm in his eyes,
he seeks shelter with the angels in mine.

Solitude

Excuse me

while I walk away from the mindless,

numbing chatter

and resume a relationship

with my true love,

Solitude.

Laughter

You're not laughing enough and life is getting shorter and shorter. This is a problem we need to work on. Come with me. Let's run crazy. Let's be spontaneous, adventurous, wild...I know I can make you smile again. I know there is happiness sitting inside your amazing soul just waiting to burst. And I know I am the one to help you bring it to the surface. Laughter will save your life. Letting me love you will save mine.

Be vulnerable once in a while;
it's refreshing to see someone
so soft and brave and tender like that.

Kiss

She'll dazzle you with star love.
She'll gather all your scars
and wounds and broken parts
and kiss them all with love.

*In a world full of dirt and darkness,
she'll always be soul and starlight.*

Lunatic Girl

You're too sane
for a lunatic girl like me.
You live in reality,
while I tango
in the jungle
of my imagination
making love to
firecracker dreams.

Electric Birds

I was logical, rational, sane

and quite content,

until you came along.

You opened the chamber to my madness

releasing all those wild,

repressed,

electric birds.

On the Verge of Finding My Wings

On the verge...
of unclasping the shackles
strangling my heart,
I welcome a fresh flow
of velvet blood as it drips
from my broken
barely beating heart,
dry tears turn liquid,
waking me, cleansing me,
as they pour forth
from the pockets of my soul.
Choking on butterflies,
I am on the verge of finding my wings.

Run with Me

Run with me in the storm.

Dance with me in the wind,

until we're both frantic

and frightfully dizzy.

Let's get lost in the cumulous clouds.

I need to know...can you handle my wild,

while embracing my inner child?

Us

Put the two of us together
and we become
like fireflies and moonlight;
all burning and glowing
and lighting up the night.

Burning Star

He is dark,

his soul of midnight and madness,

but he lights up my heart like no other.

An undying fire.

Most assuredly,

we are of the same

burning star.

Magical Soul Thing

We were the glory

never to be tamed

burning immortal flames

crying no shame

making love on rooftops

in the rain

in the canyon

on the plains,

couldn't get enough

a magical soul thing.

Protected

Do not underestimate

The beast behind

Her glistening princess eyes

The dragon guarding

Her passionate heart

Or the angels

Surrounding her...always.

Soul Rubs

She craves soul rubs,

the rare kind that

linger long after

physical departure.

Halo and Horns

Just because

she sports a halo

doesn't mean

she's without horns.

A lil angel, a lil devil
Depends on the day
Depends on the moon

Moon

Got lost in the moon;

the eyes, the face,

the soul of the soul.

That's when I knew

I belonged not with the humans,

but with the wolves,

for I was in perpetual motion

with the Universe.

Ancient like the atmosphere.

Wild like nature.

The Spirit is eternal
No ending, no beginning
Only perpetual transformation

Trust

I don't trust easily
because my sixth sense
speaks loudly to me.
If I've let you in my universe,
then know
there is something there...you are
uniquely special.
Please don't take
my trust for granted.

An Almost Beautiful Love

He tried

to tame

the gypsy

in my soul

and it killed

a beautiful love

we almost had.

Earn It

As for me,
my soul is not up for grabs.
One must earn it before
being allowed entrance.

Bliss

My eyes saw you,

but damn,

did my soul

feel you.

I know a beautiful soul when I feel one.
The empath in me
honors the authentic in you.

Chaos and Peace

Some hearts crave chaos;

mine is one.

Yet my soul is a constant source of peace.

Quite the contradiction am I.

Still, I am free.

Moon Whispers

Those soft moon whispers,

gentle soul taps,

angel thoughts...Listen to them.

They are your sixth sense, your intuition.

Those still small voices have messages for you.

Trust them.

*When you wake every morning put your soul shine on,
and you just might be surprised how well your day goes!*

Sky

Don't need a magic carpet

to soar

or wings to fly.

I simply close my eyes

and place my soul

against the sky.

Love

Gaze at her the way astronomers gaze at stars.

Love her the way the moon loves the night sky.

Anything less is a waste of time.

Cellular

Because some cells are aligned on a cell level,

the Universe will stop at nothing to ensure

those invisible wires connect and catch fire.

I think my soul was born with wings;
it's always restless,
it won't sit still.

If you haven't spontaneously sashayed outside on a dark starry night, with a manic moon smiling down at you...if you haven't danced under the glorious sun, run barefoot in the woods, hugged a tree, kissed the wind, swum naked in the ocean or any outside body of water, or let snowflakes fall on your tongue until you're inhaling the sky itself, then you've been asleep...it's time you WAKE UP and get intimate with Mother Earth, and let her get intimate with you. Experience real adventure, embrace the feel of freedom, feel the magic. Cast your inhibitions aside! Life is too precious and too short to let another minute wait. Become one with the Earth. Feel the Force of Freedom. Of truly living!
Become Bohemian, if only in stolen moments.

Crashing

When it comes to matters of the heart and soul,

I'm not a falling kind of girl.

I'm more of a

Slamming

Crashing

Erupting

Bursting and Infinitely Alive

She has an electric magnetic soul.

Soul on fire,

Like fireworks on the Fourth of July.

Like sparklers igniting hearts.

Like stars exploding in the sky.

Like spontaneous combustion coursing through veins.

Like neon lights.

Like all things bursting and infinitely alive!

Journey

Got consumed in you and found myself...lost.

So, one day I took a stand and said,

"No more! It's time for me to get back to me!"

Now I am on a journey of finding myself again,

of self-discovery, a soul journey.

I am looking forward to the windy,

sometimes stormy ride,

the bumps, the grinds,

and eventually, grace that catches me along the way.

*While you were busy working on your ego,
she was busy working on her soul.*

Lost and Found

I left

you

so

I could

find

me.

The more inward I've gone,
the more me I've found.

Wild Horse

Every woman has a wild horse she keeps concealed

Like the soft energy of twilight

Like the mysterious shadows of a black, pale moon:

Veiled, hidden, tucked away.

*There lives a wild horse
in the center of every woman's soul.*

Enigma Between Breaths

Listen for the chiming of your heartbeat;

unravel its song and follow its voice.

The enigma between breaths,

the stillness...the silence,

where life and death collide,

where darkness hides.

Feel the currents, cadences, pulses, rhythms;

for these, the song of your heart,

contain the secret story of you.

Be Still

Take time to listen to what the silence is saying.
Often it is in stillness, gentleness, quietness we receive
revelation...guidance...direction. But you must pay
attention or you will not hear the tune being revealed
through the subtle, silent screams. Silence can be loud
when it has a message to convey.

~ Journey into Self ~
Traveling into the wilderness of your psyche
brings you back to your sacred self.

My Silence

Some days my silence is elaborate.

Dripping like honey from a hive,

my imagination blooms.

The landscape of my mind growing

like a pasture of wild weeds:

Untamable, unstoppable, powerful.

It is here, in the silence,

I become active, feral, confident.

In the quiet of my mind, I find great power.

Some days my silence is elaborate-

Screaming...clawing...scratching.

Soul Love

When you find your twin flame

you also find your freedom,

for there is nothing more exhilarating,

wild and free

than absolute soul love.

Reincarnated Love

He had the power to reincarnate love

in a place of pain and heartbreak.

A place void of hope. He loved her

with every cell, every fiber of his being.

And he wasn't afraid to show it.

She needed the warrior in him,

craved his fight, his dark and his light.

He proved time and again

he was her salvation.

Spaces Between Us

If I show you my flaws will you still love me?

If I take you to the depths of my soul

the abyss

where demons laugh

play

and have their way

where darkness hides

where scars and bruises stick like glue

will you look at me with the same heat in your eyes?

Will your heart still beat fast and ferocious for me?

Will you still think of me in the spaces between us?

Poet in Her Heart

You are a majestic light in a dark world.

Candles cannot flicker without a flame.

Flowers will not thrive without a sun.

Stop running from the passion in your soul.

Cease hiding in the abyss that attempts

to swallow you whole

and be the fiery flame that you are.

Be to the world the poet that lives in your heart.

I will not apologize for the flame in my soul.
Not to you. Not to anyone.
It is how I was created and who I am.

Timeless

I hold a fondness,

a deep appreciation

for rare, old souls;

those who see not

with their physical eyes,

but beyond, to a deeper level,

a realm that goes deep under the surface.

These souls are timeless, eternal,

because they know naught of age.

Feel It

You'll find magic everywhere,

even in dark, dusty corners,

if you stop searching

with your limited human eyes

and instead feel with your naked soul.

The Crazy One

I am an artist, a rebel one at that.

I live in the voluptuous dimension of imagination.

If you are expecting normalcy (dullness) from me,

sorry to disappoint, but you're quite mistaken.

Ordinary is not my best attire,

I've tried it and normal just never fit quite right.

I will always be the crazy one who believes in magic,

unicorns and impossible dreams.

But also love, compassion and empathy.

I am a romantic rebel,
living in the paradise of my making.

Heart-Centered

The mind of a poet is not politically correct.

We speak with our hearts

and write from our souls.

Beauty comes in all forms,

correct or not,

and poets break rules.

They push boundaries.

For us, listening to our hearts

is the only way to be true.

Breathtaking Depths

If you are only interested in the surface

don't waste my time.

Too shallow to realize

fascination begins

between lines,

underneath breaths,

beneath skin,

down in depths

where it's desperate and dark.

*Your eyes are an ocean and I am yearning
to swim in deep, dark places.*

Vibes

No longer do I waste time

or energy enduring small talk,

lack of connection, lack of soul vibration.

Instant gratification is not my cup of joy.

If we don't have that vibe, we just don't have it

and life is too valuable to spend precious moments

pretending or trying to make something fit that doesn't.

Soul Plugs

Some days my intuition yells so loudly,

I need to wear soul plugs to drown out the screams.

Not a Stranger

You were a stranger

only by physicality.

My soul felt you immediately

and my heart intuitively responded...

a connection transcending

time and space.

~ Heart Erection ~
I need a soul connection
for a heart erection.

Resisting the Artist

Resisting the artist, the creative inclinations and tune of your being will only drive you to insanity's edge. Feel the flow of passion's rage – let it lead the way. You are an artist, a creator, dancing to your soul's unique rhythm. You have no business denying what's natural. Instead, obey your calling. The proclivity to make art, to create: it's a gift. A gift that is rightfully yours.

*The moon
has taken
residence
inside my
wildflower
soul.*

Angels in the Flesh

I love it when you meet an angel on Earth

and they have no idea that's what they are;

a human angel, an angel covered in skin.

They are the best kinds of humans to know.

As your eyes widen,

as you evolve and your soul is receptive,

you will encounter and recognize these angels

on Earth more and more.

Dark Spaces

Just because your eyes are not brave enough

to meet her in the dark

doesn't mean

she is lost.

Rather,

your soul is weak,

unable to adjust

to the black of midnight.

Too dim to see

beauty in darkness.

Perhaps you're afraid of her clandestine essence,

her radiance, her charm,

too cowardly to explore deep,

dark spaces.

Soul Illumination

If you can find magic in my broken spots,

glitter behind my sad eyes,

secrets my spirit hides,

then my love,

I do believe

you are on your way

to unweaving

the knots in my heart

and illuminating my soul.

Stories

There are stories inside your eyes.

Chapters underneath,

below and above your eyes.

Secrets and lies

and truths disguised.

Unafraid

Because he was not afraid of the breaths of my soul,

The torments of my inner sanctuary,

He found me there,

He loved me there-

The flaws, the scars, the moon and the sun,

All of me.

Completely.

He did not merely love me in parts.

And it was there, in our vulnerabilities,

Masks pulled away,

That we touched.

Our love was deeper than love:

It was not of this world, time or place.

Open and Find

Close your mouth
and open your mind.
Lose your self
and find your soul.

*I want your naked soul
or nothing at all.*

Rhythm

Expectations always fucked me in the end. These days, I live, breathe and move freely with the rhythm of my soul and the beat of my heart...no longer driven by fake friends with their false truths, false doctrines or any-one's expectations. I'm just being me, and if that's not enough for you that's also fine by me.

Scream and Claw

That hiss, that noise,

that pounding in your head!

If you're feeling a persistent nag in your gut

you must absolutely pursue it.

Only the soul will scream and claw

incessantly to get your attention.

I call that Passion,

and Passion must have its way

or it will eat you to death,

burning you from the inside out,

leaving you standing, empty

in your own pit of ashes.

~ Reach Inside ~
You only taste the blood of your soul
by cracking open
and reaching into the abyss.

Fire is My Serenity

I immerse myself in chaos
like "normal" people immerse
themselves in routine.
I crave primal living,
for this is where I develop
my craft, my art.
This is where I'm truly alive.
In the fire, I find serenity
and feel almost complete.

Don't Need You to Fly

You thought you could

twist me up,

tie down my wings,

screw with my heart,

but darling, you forgot,

I am fucking flexible!

Nothing you do or say

could keep me bound.

I'm connected to the sky.

I don't need you to fly.

She's her own empire,
with
or without you.

Grace

Stones tossed in my direction and you're there always

Your angelic wings covering me in protection

Your still small voice speaking silently

of comfort and love

Your gentle grace guiding me

Peace pouring over me,

washing me clean.

Be mindful of angels
guiding and guarding your path.
Walk with them.

Staying Afloat

It's okay if I don't understand everything

or have it all figured out.

I'm not trying to save the world.

I'm just trying not to drown in it

~ Spaces ~
We are all just humans trying to survive in this crazy world,
in the spaces between birth and death.

Soul Seeker

When you're a soul seeker, you question, you wonder, learn, evolve. We stretch and ultimately outgrow things – ways of thinking, philosophies, objects, even people – that once seemed vital in our lives. As searchers, it's crucial we step away for a time (sometimes forever). Your soul will speak to you, if you listen, and you'll know what you need to know WHEN you need to know. You'll return with a freshly invigorated perspective. Whatever your soul is doing, let it move forward at its own pace, with its own rhythm. You will return to yourself with renewed vitality and the answers you were awaiting. Even answers to questions you didn't know you had, but your heart knew, and the time away gave your soul the rest and peace it needed to find clarity. This will make you a better person to those around you, society and ultimately the world. Allow your essence to speak....be patient with yourself while you bloom. Out of the box thinking indeed...exactly what soul seekers should always be striving for. Go with your heart and your soul, whatever they speak...they know the way.

Reclaim Your Crown

Be kind to yourself by releasing self-made, self-inflicted drama. Never forget, you're a shining star, radiating brilliance from the inside out. Warrior king. Warrior queen. Do not diminish your power by allowing regrets, resentments, anger, shame, guilt, fault-finding to take up your brain space and eat your insides. You simply must let those lower frequencies go, else you stay shackled, while lowly energy vibrations fester like maggots. Reclaim your crown and find your freedom.

The princess needs a prince, while the queen became bored babysitting the king and realized he adds unnecessary stress to her already busy life.

The Queen Will Teach the King

He said he wanted to make me his queen.

I said, "Darling, I don't need a king to be a queen.

I am already a queen, with or without you.

I have my own throne and my own kingdom,

inside of me.

Follow me...I'll lead you into my royal castle.

I'll show you my mental sanctuary

filled with treasures of the mind, heart and soul,

and I'll teach you how to find

your own inner jewels and gems

to which silver and gold could never compare."

~ *Lioness* ~
If you aren't aware,
there is a lioness living inside you.
Maybe it's time you get acquainted.

Warriors

We are all warriors in this mad, mixed up world,

that is a certainty;

we just haven't all figured that out yet.

Find your warrior spirit,

your warrior strength,

and proudly put on your warrior coat.

Conquer your demons

and charge onward.

Be who you were created to be.

Be gentle with yourself while healing.
And be prepared for great strength.

Phoenix

Wake up wild one!

Your mind is a cageless bird

waiting to fly to unchartered lands.

Like the phoenix,

you will rise again with renewed vigor,

clarity, compassion and insight.

Shedding Old Skin

I am shedding my old skin to allow new growth.

There's a new layer of depth, strength and badass

blooming from within.

I let go of toxicity, aware of poisonous dragons

that would fight and try taking me down

to their meager level in the ground.

I refuse, dirt is not my playground.

Hell is not my home.

~ Inner Fortune ~
Be so filled with inner glorious moonlight
to forbid bullshit and drama sneaking in the back door.
Keep the poison out,
and the love and star glitter flowing in.

You Are Every Season

You can sit wallowing in regrets, the mistakes you've made, stumbles you've had, or you can look at your mishaps as colorful adventures on life's highway. All your experiences have shaped and strengthened you into the unique warrior that you are. You have evolved into a beautiful vibrant strong wise compassionate human being!

You are learning to accept your flaws, your chaos, your screw-ups. You're glorious and radiant, more powerful than you realize. You are an ever-blooming flower. You are moonlight. You are every season. You're love personified. You, my dear, have truly lived and you are more delightfully beautiful for it. If someone hasn't told you this lately, I am here to tell you now.

Mending

Your brokenness will strengthen you.

Every fiber of you!

It doesn't seem so,

especially in the currents of being ripped apart,

but in the mending,

we are made more durable, stronger.

External events beyond your control;
Refuse to give them power - let them go.

Feral Flame

Don't let little minds
and judgmental tripe
ruin your tranquility
or disturb your inner sanctuary.
You're a golden heart and a feral flame,
and that's a beautifully glorious thing.
Stay true to YOU!

Love is Life

 Allowing fear to destroy the possibility of love is a travesty. You may lose your head, your heart may bleed. There is no guarantee in love, so you put up a shield to guard your heart from Cupid's arrow, instead of opening to the infinite flow love offers. You purge life and choose death, for a life without love is death, enslavement. You chose to live in chains, while I chose freedom. I have no use for timid hearts. I'll take the flame, the fire, the burn. Love is freedom. I'll go out with a bang and a boom! Love is immortal. Love is life. If my heart pumps bleeding tears, if I go mad with jilted love, if my body is ravished with love's passionate embrace, at least I chose life. We all die in the end anyway, but I refuse shallow living, to die with a puny, lifeless heart. I refuse to give up one second of freedom for a life of slavery to my own past and limited fears. I reject fear's trap.

Acceptance

You can be both wild and tame,

enjoy pleasure and pain.

You can have overflowing love in your heart,

light in your eyes, heat in your veins.

There is no correct way or wrong way.

We are adventurers passing through life's highway.

Our journey is about accepting the dark and the light,

learning to love ourselves where we are,

flaws and all.

Accepting and not judging ourselves or others.

Be yourself above all else

and by the way of Universal design,

all will fall into place and be as it should.

Opposing Energies
Clarify and Connect Us

There is a beautiful,

spacious and binding connection

between our light and dark sides.

Don't fear either one.

We are a complexity of both light and dark,

two different energies, yet bound together,

and the balance between both is breathtaking,

almost mystical.

It is in our own darkness that clarity emerges

and our path illuminates.

Without the darkness

we are incapable of searching deep

within ourselves to discover,

often unknowingly and accidentally,

all the glorious light we hold within.

Each of us.

The Heart

The heart is strong, a powerful force

to be reckoned with.

It pumps and pounds 24/7.

Powerful, durable, sturdy – created that way.

Your heart may break;

it may rip and tear along the way, at times

feel as though a blade is ripping it apart.

But that beautiful bloody organ,

my dear,

keeps performing, functioning,

as it's meant to do.

Remember that, my love,

when your heart is hurting

and you think you can't go on.

You can! You always can!

Glass Heart

My heart was like glass,

breaking into tiny

sharp pieces.

Somehow the memories all stayed in place,

together in the soft tissue of my center.

And I smiled knowing how fortunate I was

to once have had such a powerful love,

a pleasure and pain

that will always remain

running thick through my veins.

Storms

Be with someone
who willingly runs
in the storm with you,
not someone who cowers away
because of turbulent winds.

Heat and Electricity

Don't get attached to her

If you are fearful of fire and lightning

Or if thunder is too loud

For your timid soul

She is heat

Electricity

Always brewing

She plays with violent flames

And dances in glorious storms.

Madness

I don't fear the madness that springs forth,
occasionally devouring me.
I'm ready to cut the crazy wide open
and explore it more vigorously.

Embracing

Exquisite art

often emerges from the most tormented minds

and dark imaginations.

From the ashes, beauty rises.

In the dirt, seeds bloom to life,

into vibrant flowers.

In the darkness

stars shine brightest.

Embrace the night of your being,

for this is where your light lives.

A plethora of mystery and beauty

haunting your dark inner landscape.

Genius in Crazy

Where there's madness, there's genius.

Where there is genius, there's creativity.

We all have it somewhere within us;

that hint of madness,

spark of genius,

untapped creativity.

Devil's Counterclaim

I'm always playing devil's advocate in my head,

which gets so damn exhausting,

but the devil...she just won't shut up.

Moon, Madness, Hands and Teeth

Sometimes,

the only things in this world

that make sense

are the moon,

my madness

and your hands messing up my hair,

while your teeth sink into my soul.

Ravenous

Do not blame my heart's appetite
for how it chooses to feast,
for my heart is a wild lover,
an all-consuming beast.

Eternal Darkness

He wasn't like a moth

attracted to her flame.

No,

he was like a vampire,

in love

with her eternal darkness.

Obsession

I love with an obsession that borders insanity.

If you become my victim,

please know I hold little control

where my heart may go,

but here is a guarantee:

I will take you to wild places-

We will have grand and wicked adventures.

You will experience a love like no other,

because if you become my object of desire,

like the sky,

my heart has no limits.

Forbidden

He thrived on her dark intensity,

her tumultuous insanity,

her passionate originality.

She was a hunger he couldn't fill,

a craving he couldn't tame.

Her soul collided

with his ravenous appetite

and he couldn't get enough!

She was his forever decadent,

secret addiction.

Beast in My Bed

You were the beast in my bed;

the wild lover,

never meant to stay,

never meant to tame.

But only YOU understood the howling chaos

of my soul,

and now we live apart,

and every night

I seek solace from the moon.

Insomniac Artist

My mind won't deactivate

at night like it should,

as a normal person's mind would.

So, like a madness driven by the moon,

I scribble and write,

with ink do I fight,

turning words into rhyme

and tears into flow,

until the blood of my heart

is scripted in art.

Fangs

Never ask a writer

what they are writing

while they are writing,

unless you're prepared

for sharp teeth,

fangs

and blood on your lap.

Corpse

(Sylvia Plath inspiration)

As I lay like a corpse

in this dreamy

insomniac dimension,

I spit quotes

out of thin air

and pluck strands

from my red hair.

Burning Moon

Beware,

the moon is ablaze tonight.

no telling what kind of

insanity she'll ignite.

Listen to the wolves howl.

Oh my,

her highness is on the prowl.

2 a.m. Fleshly Words

Greedy lovely beast

who consumed my heart,

devoured my soul,

and left me with a madness;

a wicked devil's tongue.

Now I write you in my 2 a.m. poems,

and savor every fleshly word.

Vine

Your love was a vine,

Enchanting and beautiful

Crawling around my heart

And up my throat

Then it strangled me

Your love,

Hauntingly tragic.

My Perfect Storm

He was my perfect storm,

the kind of tornado my mind, body and soul craved.

I was his dreamy bohemian poet,

his perfect melodic muse.

He took my flaws and made them into virtues.

I took his dark crimson heart

and made it into burning love.

He fell in love with this unpredictable primal creature.

And I fell in love with everything about him.

Binocular Eyes

Those eyes startled me

I swear they saw straight

to the core of my fractured,

hungry,

wild soul.

Thunder

If you don't like storms

and aren't prepared for hurricanes,

better stay away from her calm seas,

for lightening courses through her lovely blue veins

and underneath that soft exterior roars thunder.

~ *Deception* ~
She appears quiet and subdued.
The paradox:
Raging storms twirl inside her.

Mad Stars

Poetry foams on the tongue,

dripping from lips,

as art flows off fingertips.

Have no fear of lightning bolts in your eyes

or mad stars dangling down your cheeks.

Welcome the insanity. Enjoy the ride.

Life is short,

make it about things

that bring you to life;

otherwise you'll walk around in a shell

with a heartbeat,

dead inside.

Danger does not intimidate me.
What frightens me most is feeling dead,
while having a pulse.

Venom

There is something stirring within.

Not sure what it is but it's black and blistery

scratching my lily white skin.

I am drawn to poison, the beast – him.

His hunger, his pleasure.

My poison, my sin.

If I choke or if I die, you'll know

his alluring venom is the reason why.

He fed my aching heart deceit when it was hungry,

incomplete.

He cleansed me with freshly baked lies,

which I devoured reluctantly, yet eagerly;

the craving lacks sufficient control.

This pleasure, this pain—

Tempestuous, difficult to refrain.

Spectacular Unfoldment, for Eyes that See

Where you see sad eyes,

I see dazzling darkness.

What you perceive as gloom,

I perceive as glorious madness.

What you think is lost is only misplaced.

You see chaos.

I see an enchanting wild forest.

Dreams. Possibilities.

Sometime spectacular in the making.

She has a quiet voice and a loud mind.
Her eyes reflect an internal shine,
her heart's divine

Counterparts, Twin Flames

She was the storm,

could be found by the sea,

sometimes lost in the tides.

He was the calm,

gently embracing her currents,

guiding her back to shore.

She, secure in his infinite love.

Sanity

You drive me crazy,

but

you keep me

sane.

Red Headed Hurricane

Telling a red headed storm to chill

is like telling the ocean to stop making waves.

I'm the sea,

the storm,

the center,

the calm.

In the middle of my tornado

let me roll, let me rumble.

My intensity makes me who I am.

My ferocity grounds me.

Eternity

His eyes were the sea;

gentle and vast,

alive and turbulent,

crashing violent waves into her heart.

Her eyes were magic;

full of the moon,

starlight,

everything lovely and bright.

Together they collided,

souls entwining,

eternity unfolding.

Crimson and Fire

On a steamy summer night
she drinks chilled white wine,
writes introspective prose
and menacing poems.
She sits in absorbed stillness
savoring her aloneness.
A shattered heart of crimson afflicts her,
but don't let this solemn poetess fool you
She's a wicked wild tigress,
with forest fires flowing in her veins.

Dark Devotion

Promise me you'll stay
and I promise to haunt you
in the most heavenly way,
with dark devotion
and deep emotion.

Wall of China

She may seem closed off,

guard up,

Wall of China around her,

but really

she wants you to liberate the guard,

shatter the wall,

and unravel her madly.

You Have Super Powers

So you love harder than them and feel deeper than
most. Why do you insist that's a weakness when in fact
it's a fucking super power—magical! Count your
blessings, you could be a cold fish—bitter, hard, callous.
There's no grandeur in not feeling deeply and loving
passionately. Your tenderness is your greatest strength.
Your softness allows you to feel, empathize,
and be intuitive. You have more power than you know.

Phases

Some nights

you're a starless sky;

void, black, empty.

But the moon never abandons,

even on its shyest nights

tucked away behind dark clouds

the moon refuses to leave.

And you'll be vibrant with life again,

shining bright soul light

to a dim world.

Be patient like the moon.

You are a beautiful light in a dark world.

Sanctuary, Serenity

Those dark, forbidden places;

They offer me refuge and sanctuary.

Peace and tranquility.

Darkness is my serenity.

I think I would asphyxiate in all your light.
I need my darkness...I need my madness.

Bright Star

She's far from ordinary;

she's a rare breed,

a black rose,

a deep soul,

a gypsy heart,

a bright star.

Or you could simply say,

she's magic.

Part Angel, Part She-Wolf

She wasn't the type of girl to get consumed

in herd mentality.

She was a solitary beauty,

quite other-worldly,

with her own sets of ideas and personal philosophies,

shining her inner luna light

and dancing her own soul rhythm.

She never required the masses

to dictate her thoughts or movements.

She was a lone warrior.

I'm convinced part angel, part she-wolf.

Big Bad Wolf

The big bad wolf came to her in hopes

of devouring her pretty little soul

and feasting on that tender exuberant heart of hers.

Instead of trembling and trampling fearfully away,

she embraced the beast

with all his beautiful imperfections

and flawless features...and fell desperately,

madly, marvelously in love!

Clandestine Ways

She often writes dark, forbidden poems, too menacing for the masses. Her spirit is wild and free. A brave and beautiful black swan, too deep to wade with the flock. A feral she-wolf, independent of the pack. But she loves, oh does she love, only free souls like her truly understand how to give and receive pure unadulterated love. Run courageously with her in the wind and you'll find your heartbeat in sync with the earth and the sky.

~Moon Child~
The moon beckons me.
The wolves call my name.
I am made for the night,
a creature of the dark
where my soul can breathe
and my spirit can play.

Wolf Blood

I have wolf blood

and wolf bones.

Don't expect me

to graze with sheep.

Save the drama
for the queens.
Stand alone
be a wolf,
a rebel,
a warrior,
a savage,
a badass.
Be anything
but a damn
drama queen!

Rise

Rise to the challenge of being the wolf that you are

Strong, confident, secure in you

Not perfect, yet perfectly imperfect

Committed to a constant upward flow

Refrain from lowly thinking

Strive for betterment in all your ways

Less judging, more accepting

That's huge. That's power.

That's the wolf in YOU!

My Gypsy Jane

She walks barefoot in the woods.

Always returns smelling like a wildflower

and howling like a wolf.

My Gypsy Jane.

Played

Even wolves let their guard down from time to time

and become a hunter's favorite game.

Hunted.

Captured.

Deceived.

Betrayed.

Renaissance Warrior

She gathers strength and wisdom from trees

where she's rooted in perfect harmony,

fearless of bees or anything feral and free.

The pathless forest is her home,

sheltered comfort is not her zone.

She sports black medieval boots,

romping in the thick weeded woods

playing hide and seek with the forest nymphs.

Barefoot

Sometimes one needs to run
barefoot in a field of wildflowers...or any
kind of flowers!
And feel the earth under their feet,
the wind on their face,
and the sun on their hair to realize
how grounded and blessed they truly are.
Hug a tree. Hell, kiss the tree!
Lay on the grass...or the dirt.
Jump on piles of leaves,
roll down hills...remember when you did that as a kid!?
Dancing under the clouds,
under rainbows and baby blue skies
is like massaging Mother Earth.
Nature loves you,
especially the wild child in you,
and when you love her back
she'll reward you abundantly.

Dust

Let the dust accumulate.

You have stories to tell,

adventures waiting,

life to love,

love to share.

The dust can wait.

Mischief and Madness

She's mischief and madness
waiting to catch fire
and set souls ablaze;
fluttering in the wind,
impishly making violet love
under a sapphire moon.

Dash of Divinity

She'll crawl into your soul

like a forbidden love,

leaving you breathless

as you sink

into her holy darkness and

radiant aura of her essence.

Mesmerized, hypnotized—

She's a little bit witch-woman

Dash of divinity

Heaven and hell.

Witch

Her wings have been clipped for centuries,

yet she still takes flight at night

when the moon is full and bright.

She is nocturnal
The moon is her guide
She runs with wolves
The howl is her cry

Winter

Solitude

Creeps into my bones like winter.

Slowly

Steadily

Suddenly

Like the cold and the dark.

I am alone, but I am not lonely.

The Darkness is My Lover

I write about the dark because it knows me well.

I am Winter. I am Cold.

I breathe in black

and exhale gold.

My heart is pure,

my heart is true;

still, it's been bruised by quite a few.

Got knives lodged in me older than you.

Indestructible

You may have damaged her edges, fractured her trust, shattered her heart, but darling, you could never come close to destroying her kind soul and loving spirit, for she is a creature of the Gods, inhabitant of the angels. Pure. Made of shimmering moonlight and breathtaking heavenly wings. You could never destroy a spirit like her. Try as you might, she is covered with strength...angelic wings of protection always encompassing her. Mother Goddess rises in her with beauty, grace and love. She is indestructible to your evil kind.

Karma

I'm sorry your heart was split open

and for all the pain

you're now enduring,

but honey,

perhaps karma has made her way

back to you.

Wild Child

Always the wild child,

conceived in flames,

born of fire.

Drawn to the forbidden,

witch, warlock, burning stones.

Her blood is made of moonlight;

part dark, part light.

Her heart, it's a sword;

fiercely loyal and will fight

to the death for those whom she loves.

You can throw her in the fire,

she always returns as the flame—

the fervor is her anchor,

her safe-haven and her blood.

I Am Not

I am not like those other women

bowing down to the whims

of insecure, domineering men.

I am a bird, a raven, a witch, an angel.

I fly to the sound of my heartbeat.

Mother Goddess is my Guide.

The Universe is my voice.

Telepathic Lover

Telepathic lover

Come to me

I am burning

Desperately.

Bloody Swoon

The ravenous, rabid poet

awaits

the midnight moon.

She'll trick

and out wit

her unsuspecting lover,

the beginning of a bloody swoon.

Constellations

She dances

under a glistening

golden sky

Dangerous and wild!

Her hair smells of fire

and ashes,

while her eyes are

full of constellations.

In the night,
I wake and come to life.
Blame it on my dark heart.

The Spell

Don't ever uncast

the spell

you have

on me.

Linger a little longer on my lips love,
let me drink you all in.

Magnet

It's the midnight flicker in her eyes
and the mystery of her rapacious-looking mouth
that draw them like a magnet to her heart.

Pendulum

My heart is a fevered,

pulsing pendulum;

it aches and beats

back and forth,

between

the silver shadow of the moon

and crashing expanse of the sea.

And like an eclipse,

my heart is a shadow,

and then the dark.

Bourbon

He was a late night

shot of bourbon

the taste of him

left me burning

with mouth on fire

body full of desire.

~ Inferno ~

I thrived on his fire

He lived for my madness

My dirty kisses

We were undying fervor

Dancing volcanoes erupting in lust

Love and all things in between

Together, we moved mountains

Together, we were invincible

Welcome to Wonderland

He unlocked the gate to the darkest part of his soul, the part hidden from the world, and welcomed me to his entire Kingdom. He released the bolt lifting the steel chamber that protected my heart for so long, because with him hiding was no longer necessary, guarding was pointless...I was free...to be me, entirely and truly to the darkest fiercest root, to the brightest beam of light...to become the queen of his throne, the ruler of his joy. We loved beyond comprehension, in the light and the dark, under blue and purple moons and rainbows of fire. We were the mates to our souls. He was my King, I his Queen, in his Wonderland where he took me, kissed me and loved me, all of me, every day, tirelessly,
relentlessly, protecting me, reassuring me I was his heart, and he was mine. I was Kingdom. He was my Throne...with vows until the end of time.

Demons and Perfect Love

The demons, they return to haunt the crimp in my heart.
No amount of burning herbs, or magic spells and bitter
potions cast the beasts away. Garlic rosaries won't
remove the black infection slowly devouring within.
Only love, perfect love, casts out the monsters and the
fiends that invade like a thief in the night infecting and
destroying, attempting to steal my joy. But love is life
and I choose life. I choose love. Throw away the herbs,
release the spells, let me swallow love's divinity.

Madness

The amount of her madness

depends on the amount of her love.

If she is crazy, frantic, insane with you,

then simply stated . . .

She is in love with you.

Aphrodisiacs

Genuine soul connections
are the real aphrodisiacs.

Gravitational Pull

It began with his mind, that midnight paradise—

Primal. Feral. Wicked.

Then I heard his...husky masculinity

His honey-dripping voice

became my gravitational pull.

One word from his remarkable,

beautifully lascivious lips

and there befell a force

beyond my control.

Suddenly

Suddenly, I couldn't turn away

from his piecing, infectious gaze.

He was wrong and tragic and gorgeous

all at the same time.

At that moment, I understood how alike we were,

that he belonged with me,

and I with him.

Mountains Move, Ground Shakes, Stars Tumble

They say mountains don't really move

when you fall in love.

I don't believe them,

because I swear I saw mountains move

the moment I fell in love with you.

And I swear I feel the ground shake

every single time we touch.

And when we kiss,

hot liquid stars tumble from the sky,

searing my skin.

Don't tell me there is no such thing as magic.

Our love has proven them wrong.

Love Sublime

He doesn't love me in an ordinary fashion,

with flower petals and saccharine words.

He loves me sublimely,

dirty words and filthy thoughts.

He fists my hair and pushes me down.

He grabs my face, he tastes my lips,

devouring me with venom kisses and vampire bites.

That's how he loves me;

Recklessly, yet lovingly,

down to the depths and desperateness

of my lonely bones.

He understands me: my needs, my hungers,

my cravings, desires.

He is the only one who has ever gotten to my core,

my soul!

He completes me,

makes me holy.

Cinder and crimson unite,

infinite combustion.

Teasing Tongues

Teasing tongues

Twisted Sheets

Tangled in love

Those are about the only things

Tidy and proper

This morning.

Beyond

We were not of this world—

Dancing with fireflies

we lit up the night sky

embracing the darkness and light within each other.

We tasted of salt and earth and flesh.

He dissolved in me,

while I melted with him.

Together, he and I became intensity,

perfect insanity.

Ethereal, eternal, omnipotent, limitless—

We loved beyond this world.

He Loved Me

He loved me until my bones bled,

then he loved some more.

He loved me in the depths of hell;

He loved me there first,

before anywhere else

and

I've never felt a love, a force,

as powerful,

as complete.

~ *Love* ~
At this moment, we are one and the same -
one soul inhabiting two bodies.

Unhinged

Without you, I am unhinged

Your voluptuous mind is red velvet to my soul

Your tender touch, your prodding tongue

Igniting the woman beast in me

Our primal urges and animal instincts

Our connection like electricity

I need you like a book needs a spine

As a butterfly needs wings to fly

I crave you like the moon craves the night

Every cell in my body aches without you

Oh, what sweet agony!

My Center

I wanted to punch something.

Wanted to scream.

Wanted to run away.

Instead, I went to my center,

my heart,

where I purged my raging emotions.

I pleaded for answers,

when suddenly a gentle calm

washed over me.

Love wrapping limbs around me,

I found an inner peace.

Serenity. All within.

*You will find all the riches you ever need
in the center of your heart.
Go there. Explore.*

Topography

Purging you from my heart

is like a junkie in detox:

utterly painful.

You are rooted in my marrow,

flowing in my veins.

You are the topography of my soul.

*The blade of loving you
is what will kill me in the end.*

Unloving the Devil

It's easy to un-love the devil;

Remind yourself all he ever was, all he will ever be.

A Jekyll. A Poison.

Heart the color of the blackest night.

A tongue full of wicked lies and tasteless deception.

Teeth ready to tear into his next victim's heart.

He gave me wild kisses
and left me with ashes.
The taste of him
still scorches my mouth,
my lips, my tongue.

The Monster

She saw the monster in him but she stayed anyway. Thinking...rationalizing...praying...if she could love those hideous parts, so cleverly hidden from the masses, the cold-blooded beast, the frigid demonic-like heart, the ice would thaw and underneath there might be warmth and light. But a monster is a monster, no matter how many angels cross his path. You can dress them, disguise their beastly horns, but at the end of the day, with masks stripped away, they remain what they've always been and always will be – heartless. Ruin and destruction is the only way they play. Demons won't be kept at bay.

He is the shadow that follows me into dark places.

She Was the Night

She was the night,

in love with the stars,

always chasing the moon.

He was an early cup of coffee,

in love with her wild ocean breeze,

her mischievous ways,

her childish play.

Omnipotent Love

He loved her like a roaring lion,

even when she was most unlovable,

and there's a lot to be said for that...

that kind of fierce, raging, omnipotent love.

Love at First Bite

It wasn't her hypnotic eyes that drew him in

or the wild sway of her hips;

it was that devil's blood-red lipstick

smeared all over her chubby angel lips.

He shivered with the magnitude

of impending heaven and hell in one woman.

He crashed into heaven

while crossing the thresholds of hell.

~ Intensity ~
Her intensity drove me over the edge.
Her eyes, burning crazy like an inferno,
brought out the madman in me.
She was danger and I wanted in.

My Greatest Inspiration

I am simply a complicated girl

Mesmerized by mystery

Enchanted with shadows

Intrigued by glitter and gray in each of us

A girl fascinated with word-play;

Paradoxes, ironies, conundrums

In love with adventure and curious about the world

A girl who feels and dreams deeply

Loves passionately

Lives recklessly

But about all else, I am a girl insanely in love with you!

You are my greatest inspiration!

You taste like
Strawberry stars
On my lips.

You Taste of Poetry

With you,

Every kiss is a poem

Every touch is narrative prose

Our love is an unending saga

Infinite

Eternal.

Night Rose

Night time
You'll find her there
Blooming
Like a night rose.

Galaxy of Starlight

She's a galaxy of bright hues,

and her heart contains

a universe of love.

She is starlight.

Dance of Fireflies

Fireflies, to me, are nighttime butterflies,

Dazzling the night with magical flashes of light.

When I see these teeny tiny sparks dart in the night,

I am overcome with a sense of comfort and calm,

Same as when a butterfly flutters

around me during the day.

I'm drawn to the dance of both astonishing critters.

They remind me of life.

They remind me of hope.

We Are Art

Art is so many different things

Our lives should be art—

What we do, how we speak,

how we think, how we create,

how and what we feel,

how we see the world,

what we do with our God-given gifts.

It's all art,

just not in the conventional sense.

We are art.

Exquisite Masterpiece

You are an exquisite masterpiece,

created from the stars, the sun,

the sea and the moon.

And that is one hell of a

colossal cosmic collaboration!

Rare Rose

She's not particularly fond of red roses;

too common, unoriginal, everyday-ish,

but give her the rare rose, black or blue,

to complement her melancholy spirit and dark soul

and she lights up

like the brightest star on the darkest night.

Wild and Free

Hair tangled with the wind

Sun kissed face

Lover of the forest

the sea

the sky

and anything wild and free

She's a gypsy goddess.

Sun

She burns like the sun

Beautiful when she comes undone

No restraints

Pure passion flowing through her veins

Madness refusing to be tamed.

Bring Flowers and Cakes

Don't bring confusion to my table.
Bring flowers. Bring books. Bring cakes.
But leave your indecisiveness behind.
My heart is not up for breaking (again)
and my time is precious.
Don't waste either on murky thoughts
and cloudy thinking.

Beware the One Who Says
You Read Too Much Poetry

He told me I had too many books, how would I ever read them all! I looked at him for the monkey lunatic I suddenly realized he was, and politely told him it was time for him to go...back to whatever jungle from which he came. How foolish of me to let him into my intellectual sanctuary. A girl like me, who lives for adventure, mindgasms, fairytales and soul stimulation have too many books? Read too much poetry? Pffff!

The Initial Hook

Take her on a date to a book store—So she may get a better idea of who you are...to see your expressions while perusing the classics, poetry, erotica. She needs to see how you react to books she adores. Will your eyes light up when she asks you to read to her some more? She wants to experience how you taste your words. She wants to know if you get lost in different worlds and if you find magic when you gaze into a book. For her, this will be the initial hook.

Symphonies in the Sky

Storms,

those whirlwinds and symphonies

in the sky,

nourish her midnight soul

and comfort her gypsy spirit.

Those tempests amplify

the starlight in her eyes,

the moonbeams in her veins.

Seduced by the Sea

My hair smells of oceanic wind

My eyes are two starfish

The charming, turquoise sea

is seducing me

The rhythms of the calming

Crashing waves are my guide

Omnipotent, almost holy

They seek to cleanse my polluted soul

Here, by the seductive sea

I am unshackled. I am free.

I am me.

Third Eye

Learn to use your third eye
and you'll be able to see beyond the sky.
There is no limit,
except that which you
impose upon yourself.

Whiskey and Wine

You drink your whiskey,

I'll drink my wine.

Later when we're fevered and tipsy

we'll make savage love divine.

Until then,

let's swim in the warm, opal sea of each other.

Crash a few innocent waves,

skinny dip, laugh and get lost in those

blood-pumping hearts,

and for a time

forget all our broken parts.

Shatter Baby!

When you shattered her, oh how you allowed all kinds of free-flowing magical rainbow light to enter. You allowed a cleansing. A purification. Who would've known breaking could be so damn beautiful! I say, break baby. Let the shattered pieces split you wide open and let light enter through all cracks and crevices.

~Explosion~
Exploding into a million little pieces of stardust,
you light up the darkness in my soul.

Stop Running

You don't shine in the light, so why keep running from what makes you gloriously radiant? To deny darkness within you is to deny the magical sparkly intuitive rainbow of light that lives and moves inside your essence. One does not exist without the other. Stop running from that part of your soul and start letting your starlight glitter!

I don't trust anyone who hides
in the light denying darkness exists.

Intoxicate Me

Intoxicate me with the beauty

and breath of your soul.

Leave such imprints on my heart

that you come to me in dreams,

and I will leave you with eternal light,

cherishing you until the end of time

through synchronicity,

through poetry,

through mystery

and undeniable energy.

Healing

You keep playing with what broke you,
then wonder why you don't heal.
Leave the wound alone,
throw away the poison,
and watch the magic of recovery.
Your wings of wisdom are ready for flight.

Don't Allow

Do yourself a huge favor.

Do not allow people to sabotage your spirit

or water down your internal fire

just because they are filled with fears and insecurities.

If people are incapable of being soul lifters,

then you need to reevaluate

your relationship with them.

Perhaps those individuals aren't meant

to be a part of your life.

Some don't know better;

they are small, weak and full of fear.

Their desire is to drag you to their low level.

Don't allow it.

Do not permit thoughts of little-minded people

poison your spirit.

Don't stoop. Free yourself of negative energy vampires.

Wish them well and move on.

The Eternal Poem

I fell in love with the way he knew my words before I even spoke...the way he touched me with his deep-set eyes...the way he could see into my soul...the way he moved me like I was the earth under his feet, sky above...the eternal poem...the way his heartbeat synchronized with mine. The way he kissed me like I was the only way he could breathe...the way he embraced me like pure love. The way he possessed me like Poe

possessed

Annabel Lee

and she him.

Blooming

From the ashes

I rise.

I am blooming

into something radiant.

Disease

It's a disease, writing

Stalking its victim day and night

In the mind all the time

Words

Stories

Poems

There is no single solitary cure but to keep writing.

I'll always be the yearning poet

Bleeding ink

Chasing stars

Drunk on dreams.

The End

ACKNOWLEDGMENTS

With gratitude to those whom have led me to search inside myself and uncover glorious inner starlight: Particularly, the spirits that follow me around daily; my mom, Sheila, for your eternal optimism and always believing in me, especially when I forget to believe in me; my dad, the infinite artist, who is no longer with me physically, but absolutely with me spiritually; my family for putting up with me while I retreat to my inner world, my imagination, my writing sanctuary; my friends and writer tribe who inspire me with their own unique magic. And last, but certainly not least, my online followers and fans encouraging me with their continual cheers and feedback – you've motivated me more than you know.

~ Voice ~
In the stillness,
I reconnect and find my personal truth.
My voice.

ABOUT THE AUTHOR

Melody Lee's love of writing has been life-long.
Ever since she can remember, Melody has been writing poetry in notebooks, diaries, on scraps of paper, napkins or anywhere she can find to jot down her thoughts when inspiration strikes. Melody began sharing writing on social media in early 2016 and in that short time has acquired a large following. Early in her online writing journey, Melody's followers asked her if she had published any books of poetry, thus the seed for a book was planted. As Melody's followers continued praising her writing, vigorously sharing her work and inquiring about her books that seed grew until it blossomed into *Moon Gypsy*, an accumulation of Melody's best poetry and prose.

When Melody is not slaving for her wild writing muses or out communing with nature, she spends time with family and friends and trying new venues with her Foodies groupies, as well as advocating for animal rights and volunteering at her local Humane Society, and other charitable causes.

Melody Lee has a Bachelor of Arts degree from Florida State University and is a lifelong learner. Melody Lee resides in Florida with her husband and two sons.

You can find Melody Lee at www.facebook.com/MLPoetryJunkie; www.Instagram.com/melody_lee_poetry_junkie; and for purchases at www.etsy.com/shop/MelodyLeeEtsyStore.

Made in the USA
Middletown, DE
28 April 2022

64884272R00169